AF430659

Editing and Layout by Bob Zingmark
Illustrations by Taylor Wick
Photography by Val Zaragoza
Contributor: Justin Clark

ISBN # 9798708175939

First printing 2021

Independently publishing in USA

Authored by:
Kristine Setting Clark
kclarkallpro@gmail.com

To all those amazing feral cats, and the kind and generous people who care for them.

Callie
the Calico Cat
& Friends
The Seasons and
American Holidays
By Kristine Setting Clark Ed. D
Illustrated by: Taylor Wick

Callie
Screech
Mimi
Ginger
The
Triplets
Sebastian

Table of Contents

Table of Contents

Callie's Introduction

$\mathcal{H}$i. My name is Callie and I am a Calico cat. There are three colors in my fur: white, black and orange. I also have a crooked tail. I was born a feral cat. That means I was born outside in the wild without a home. If you look at my ears they flip up at the end, because I am part Lynx. A Lynx is a wild cat found in parts of North America and Eurasia.

My owners, Kris and Mark found and adopted me. They take good care of me and love me very much.

My best friend in the whole world is a black, feral cat named Screech. Screech has yellow eyes. We always play together. I have six other friends. Their names are Mimi, Ginger, Sebastian and The Triplets.

Miml Is a white, Siamese cat with blue eyes. She, too, was feral but was adopted by a really nice lady named Val. Val always gives us treats. We like her very much.

Ginger is yellow and white and has blue eyes.
Sebastian is black and white and sticks his tongue
out when you pet him. The Triplets are all black.
Two have yellow eyes and the third has orange eyes.
They are all feral cats. Kris and Mark make sure that
they always have food and water.

My friends and I love to play outside. Sometimes we
chase each other, wrestle or just hang out in the
warm sunshine. But what we enjoy the most are the
ever-changing seasons and the special holidays that
are celebrated throughout America.

Follow us as we run, skip, hop and jump throughout
the Winter, Spring, Summer and Fall while
celebrating America's special days.

Callie

WINTER

The first season of the year is Winter. The Winter months are December, January and February. Winter weather is very cold. In some places it even snows. In Winter the days get shorter, and the nights get longer.

I have so much fun making snow cats in the snow.

SPRING

The season following winter is Spring. The months of Spring are March, April and May. In Spring the weather begins to warm up, the flowers begin to boom and the trees begin to blossom.

I just picked a beautiful bouquet of flowers, and a butterfly and hummingbird share with me the beauty of Spring.

SUMMER

The third season is Summer.

The three months of this season are June, July and August. Summer is my favorite time of the year. The sun is nice and warm, and days are longer and the nights shorter.

Summer makes me happy.

I love to surf the warm, glassy waves of the ocean, and walk on the soft, warm sand on the beach.

FALL/AUTUMN

The fourth and last season is Fall which we sometimes call Autumn. The Fall/Autumn months are September, October and November. In the Fall, the weather becomes cooler, and the leaves on the trees turn yellow, red and orange. When the winds blow, the leaves fall off their branches, and float softly to the ground.

After the Fall season is over, Winter returns, and the seasons begin again.

Picking out pumpkins at the pumpkin patch is a lot of fun. I always try to find the biggest pumpkin to carve for Halloween.

NEW YEAR'S DAY – JANUARY 1

New Year's Day is the first day of a brand new year. Some people have parties, and some people watch college football with their friends. But one of the important things to do on New Year's Day is to make a resolution. Resolutions are promises to yourself to do things better throughout the year.

Sebastian, Mimi and I get together on New Year's Day to watch the Rose Bowl game. This year USC, the University of Southern California, is playing the Fighting Irish of Notre Dame.

MARTIN LUTHER KING, JR. DAY

Martin Luther King, Jr. fought for, and believed in the fact that everyone should be treated the same. That means no matter the color of their skin or nationality, age or disability – all are created equal.

Martin Luther King, Jr.'s "*I Have a Dream*" speech at the 1963 *March on Washington,* is one of the most famous speeches in American history.

CHINESE NEW YEAR

*T*his tradition has been around for four-thousand years. Chinese New Year is celebrated with fireworks, parades and festivals. Children receive *red envelopes* with money inside from family and friends. The envelopes have Chinese writing and pictures of fortune. They are given to the children to bring good luck.

My friends Ginger, Sebastian and Mimi
enjoy watching the colorful dragons
perform during the Chinese New Year
parade. There is so much to see!

GROUNDHOG DAY
FEBRUARY 2ND

This is the day when the groundhog comes out of its hole in the ground ending hibernation. If he sees his shadow, it is said that there will be six more weeks of Winter.

Well it looks like the groundhog has seen his shadow. Burrrr...that means there will be six more weeks of Winter!

SUPER BOWL SUNDAY

This is the annual National Football League (NFL) championship game played between the winner of the National Football Conference (NFC) and the winner of the American Football Conference (AFC). It is also a time for the fans to get together and party, and root for their favorite team.

Mimi and I watch the Super Bowl, and root for our favorite team. We also get to eat lots of goodies and treats!

VALENTINE'S DAY
FEBRUARY 14TH

Valentine's Day always falls on February 14th. It is celebrated by exchanging Valentine's Day cards with friends and family. Many cards say, "Be My Valentine." Sometimes we give and receive flowers, and big red heart-shaped boxes full of candy!

Valentine's Day is so much fun. Ginger, Sebastian and I celebrate by giving each other cards and candy hearts.

NATIONAL 'LOVE YOUR PET DAY' FEBRUARY 20TH

The purpose of this holiday is to encourage pet owners to spend more time with their pets, and show them the love and affection they deserve. My owners love me and take good care of me. This is one of my favorite holidays!

Love Your Pet Day should be every day!

PRESIDENT'S DAY
3RD MONDAY IN FEBRUARY

This holiday was first celebrated in 1885, in remembrance of our first president George Washington. It now celebrates all United States presidents.

Mimi and I celebrating President's Day. I wear a tall hat like President Abraham Lincoln, and Mimi wears a wig like George Washington.

ST. PATRICK'S DAY - MARCH 17th

*O*n this day, the Irish celebrate the birthday of St. Patrick by wearing the color green. Green is the color of Spring. If you don't wear green on this day, you may get pinched! The meal of the day is usually corned beef and cabbage. You don't have to be Irish to celebrate St. Patrick's Day. Many people wear Shamrocks, and dress like Leprechauns. You may also hear the words "Erin go Bragh," which means "Ireland Till the End of Time."

Happy St. Patrick's Day, and may you have the 'Luck of the Irish!'

APRIL FOOL'S DAY – April 1st

April Fool's Day is a tradition of playing tricks and jokes on one other. But you never want to do anything that would hurt someone.

Screech and I played a trick on Sebastian!

EASTER

Easter is a religious holiday, but it is also the day when the Easter Bunny comes to your house while you are sleeping, and hides Easter eggs, candy and other goodies for you to find. The Easter eggs are painted in beautiful, bright colors. Eggs have always been a symbol of life.

Mimi and I wear our bunny ears on Easter. We hunt for Easter eggs and chocolate bunnies, and put them in our basket.

CINCO DE MAYO – MAY 5th

*I*n English the words Cinco de Mayo mean May 5th. It's everyones' favorite Mexican holiday, a chance to listen and dance to music, eat chips and salsa, and maybe even speak some Spanish with friends. On this day in 1862, Mexico defeated the French at the Battle of Pueblo.

In the Mexican custom of sombreros and sarapes, Mimi and I wish you all a Happy Cinco De Mayo!

MOTHER'S DAY
2ND SUNDAY IN MAY

On this day we celebrate our mom for all the wonderful things she does for us. She takes care of us, she protects us, she teaches us and she is our best friend. Thanks, Mom, and Happy Mother's Day!!

This is my favorite picture of my mom
and me. Happy Mother's Day, Mom!

MEMORIAL DAY
LAST MONDAY IN MAY

Memorial Day is a time to say thank you to the men and women who gave their life to keep our country safe. Many people fly the American flag on this day, and many cities honor these people with parades and speeches.

Ginger and I place flags to remember our military people who fought so bravely for America.

FLAG DAY – JUNE 14TH

June is the beginning of my favorite season … Summer. Flag Day is the day that Americans celebrate the American flag, and all of its stars and stripes. The first flag was believed to have been made by Betsy Ross in 1777. The American flag has always stood for liberty, justice, and humanity. The 50 stars represent the 50 states, and the 13 stripes represent the original 13 colonies.

Sebastian and I fly America's flag proudly. We even have flag sunglasses!

FATHER'S DAY
3RD SUNDAY IN JUNE

*F*ather's Day is the day we thank our dad for all his love, care and affection. Dads, like moms help take care of us, and provide for us. Tell dad you love him with a Happy Father's Day card.

Happy Father's Day to my Dad.
Have a wonderful day!

INDEScription...

INDEPENDENCE DAY – JULY 4th

We celebrate Independence Day/the Fourth of July with fireworks, flags, parades and barbeques (hot dogs and hamburgers….yum!). On July 4,1776, the leaders of our country signed the Declaration of Independence. This paper declared Americans would be free, and not controlled by the British or any other country. July 4th is the birthday of our nation.

Relaxing and celebrating our country's birthday. Mimi and I are both proud to be Americats!

WOMEN'S EQUALITY DAY
AUGUST 26TH

Women were finally granted the right to vote for the first time on August 26, 1920. This bill was adopted by Congress, and became the Nineteenth Amendment to the United States Constitution. The women who fought hard to have the right to vote were called "Suffragettes."

Mimi, Sebastian, me and two of the triplets march for equality for women. The Suffragettes gave their all so women could have the right to vote.

LABOR DAY
1ST MONDAY IN SEPTEMBER

Labor Day is dedicated to the everyday worker. Labor Day is considered to be the 'last day of Summer'. We celebrate this day with picnics, barbeques, swimming and games. It makes me sad to say goodbye to Summer.

Labor Day is a day for resting, barbequing and just hanging out.

COLUMBUS DAY
INDIGENOUS PEOPLE'S DAY
2^(ND) MONDAY IN OCTOBER

Columbus Day celebrates the landing of Christopher Columbus in America. Columbus, an explorer, sailed from Spain in 1492 with three ships: the Nina, the Pinta and the Santa Maria. It is also the day which honors the Italian American heritage with parades throughout the nation.

This day is also known as Indigenous People's Day. Indigenous People's Day is a holiday that celebrates and honors Native American peoples, and commemorates their history and culture. It is celebrated throughout the United States on the second Monday in October.

Columbus sailed the ocean blue
in fourteen-hundred and ninety-two.

HALLOWEEN – OCTOBER 31ST

Halloween is one of my favorite holidays. On this day we dress up in our favorite costumes, and go door-to-door to our neighbors' homes, and when they answer the door we say "Trick or Treat." They give us candy and other treats. We carve out pumpkins, and make them into jack-o'-lanterns. They are supposed to scare away the ghosts and goblins.

It is so much fun to dress up on Halloween. Ginger is a ghost, I am a pumpkin and Mimi is a witch. We go out trick or treating with our friends.

VETERANS' DAY – NOVEMBER 11

Veterans' Day is a day to thank veterans whether living or deceased, and also active military personnel for their service to our country. These men and women serve or served in the Army, Navy, Air Force, Marines and Coast Guard. We fly the American flag proudly on this day.

Today is the day that we celebrate all those brave men and women who served our country. Thank you!

THANKSGIVING DAY
4TH THURSDAY IN NOVEMBER

Thanksgiving is the story of the early Pilgrims. The Pilgrims came to the New World, America, and were able to survive, because the Indians taught them what crops to plant and how to plant them. They also taught them how to hunt. In the Fall of 1621, the Pilgrims and the Indians sat down together in friendship, and celebrated the first Thanksgiving. Today we celebrate with turkey, stuffing, gravy, potatoes and cranberry sauce! Yum!

Sebastian and I are celebrating
Thanksgiving Day together. We are
thankful for all of our wonderful friends
and family.

CHANUKAH/HANUKKAH

Chanukah or Hanukkah is a Jewish holiday that lasts for eight days. The word, Chanukah/Hanukkah means *festival of lights.* It is celebrated nightly with the lighting of the *menorah* (a candelabra of lights/candles), special prayers and food. Children are given one present each night for eight nights. The holiday can either be in November or December or both.

Pumpkin and I are celebrating
Chanukah/Hanukkah together.

CHRISTMAS DAY – DECEMBER 25TH

Christmas is the happiest time of the year! There are decorated Christmas trees with lights, ornaments and tinsel, Christmas stockings, Christmas caroling, lots of presents and of course, Santa! But most of all, Christmas is about the birth of baby Jesus. I just love Christmas!

Sebastian, me and Ginger love the Christmas spirit. We have presents under the tree, and are getting ready to hang our stockings on the fireplace. When Santa comes down the chimney, he will leave us gifts in our stockings!

KWANZAA

*K*wanzaa was created in 1966 by Maulana Karenga. It is a week-long holiday honoring African culture, family unity and tradition and is celebrated between December 26 and January 1. Each night a different family member lights the candles, and a special word in Swahili is learned. Kwanzaa ends its celebration with a feast and the exchange of gifts. There is dancing and drumming along with the wearing of the African colors of green, red and white.

Dressed in traditional attire, the triplets
and I wish you all a very happy,
Kwanzaa!

NEW YEAR'S EVE – DECEMBER 31ST

New Year's Eve is the last day of the year. People dress up and go out to celebrate the coming of the new year. At midnight everyone says "Happy New Year." There are many parties with New Year's hats and horns. It's so much fun to spend it with family and friends and stay up till midnight.

Sebastian, me and Pumpkin are celebrating at a New Year's Eve party. It's one-minute till midnight. At 12:00, it will be a new year. Happy New Year to all!

* 9 7 9 8 7 0 8 1 7 5 9 3 9 *